Mrs. Mable R. Spear
Stevensville,
Michigan

RIV

E R S

What They Do

by

ALEXANDER L. CROSBY

and

NANCY LARRICK

Illustrated by

WILLIAM PRESTON

WHITMAN PUBLISHING COMPANY

Racine, Wisconsin

Contents

1
Changing The Earth's Face

ABOUT 150 MILLION YEARS AGO something peculiar happened along the Delaware River. It happened so slowly that the last few dinosaurs didn't notice the change. The bed of the river began to rise.

This took place where the river passed through what had once been an old mountain range. The old mountains had worn away almost entirely. They were just a few feet high on each side of the river. But now they began to rise. And they kept rising for thousands of years.

The Delaware wasn't stopped as the hard rock rose in its path. The water simply sawed its way through. For thousands of years the sand and gravel carried by the river acted like sandpaper. Stones pushed along by floods pounded the growing mountain and chipped off pieces.

The gorge that the river carved for itself has long been famous as the Delaware Water Gap. On each side the Kittatinny Mountains rise twelve hundred feet above water level. The passage is used not only by the river but also by two highways and the double track of the Lackawanna Railroad's main line from Hoboken to Buffalo.

Long before the earth had any people, rivers were changing the shape of the land. Where we live today was largely decided by rivers. Cities grew up along deep rivers. Highways and railroads followed the big streams. Farms and towns spread in the fertile valleys created by rivers.

Before the earth had its first blade of grass, rivers were making it possible for men and animals to develop millions of years later. They changed the face of our planet.

In the beginning the earth was nothing like it is today. The young world had a crust of jagged rocks around the molten rock inside. There were tall knobs, deep trenches, broad valleys. There was not a handful of soil, not a single leaf, not a drop of water, not a single mosquito. And then it began to rain. The rain probably kept up for millions of years.

Water rushed down the slopes of the bare rocks. It turned the low places into lakes and seas. As the water kept running, it wore away the rocks. Over long periods some rocks dissolved as a lump of sugar does in a cup of tea. Others were worn down by the sand and gravel carried in the rivers.

The rivers dumped most of the rock particles into the seas. But they left enough along their banks to provide soil for the first plants. Finally, as the earth cooled, the endless rains let up. Dry and sunny days became more and more common, just as in modern times.

The place where a river begins is usually a mystery. Every big river is big from the water of hundreds or even thousands of streams and smaller rivers. As you follow a river toward its headwaters it gets smaller and smaller. A river half a mile wide at its mouth will finally become a mountain stream that can be crossed with one step.

How can we tell that this brook, spilling over boulders in a ravine thick with hemlocks and maples, is the beginning of the river? We can't. The honor might just as well go to one of the other brooks that join this one a short distance down the mountain.

But even small streams have many sources. A stream may come from a marsh or pond. The marsh or pond will be fed by still smaller streams, or perhaps by two or three springs. There is no way to decide which rivulet

should bear the name of the river.

For example, the Delaware River is said to have three main tributaries: the Schuylkill, the Lehigh, and the Neversink rivers. True. But an ordinary highway map shows ninety or more tributaries, variously called creek, river, brook, or kill—and there are many smaller streams not shown on a road map.

The one sure thing is that water not soaked up by the land or evaporated by the sun will find its way to a river and eventually to an ocean. A heavy rain falls on Flourtown, Pennsylvania. Water runs from house roofs and down the driveways along East Mill Road. The gutters of the street become rivulets. At the bottom of the hill they empty into Oak Run, where dogwoods and irises make spring a beautiful thing. The stream carries surplus water from a large neighborhood past the shopping center and into Wissahickon Creek.

The creek flows into the Schuylkill River, which joins the Delaware at Philadelphia. There the millions of raindrops mix with water from New Jersey farms, from New York forests, and from Philadelphia streets. When the river reaches Delaware Bay and the Atlantic Ocean, it has come from nearly thirteen thousand square miles of countryside.

Eventually the water that rivers pour into oceans and lakes will come back as rain. Clouds will form from moisture over the oceans. Winds will carry the clouds over the land, where they will drop their moisture. Some day rivers will carry much of this rain back to the ocean. For thousands of years water has been making these endless round trips between land and sea.

2
Westward
By River
Highway

INDIANS AND BUFFALOES along the Ohio River saw strange sights in the years after the Revolutionary War. Drifting down the river came boats far larger than the canoes used by the Indians. The boats were flat with straight sides and a roof. They carried men, women, children, furniture, tools, and even horses and cows.

At night the boatmen tied up to trees by the riverbank. In the morning they poled out into the current again.

Pittsburgh, where the Ohio begins, was the place where

15

the flatboats were bought and loaded. Hundreds of emigrants came to Pittsburgh each week from the Atlantic seaboard, some bearing land grants as payment for serving in the War of Independence. Not all of the floating families found their promised land in Kentucky or Tennessee. A heavy toll of lives was taken by Shawnee Indians and river pirates along the Ohio.

Dangerous though the trip was, the Ohio was the only good highway to the West. Some hardy frontiersmen chose the Wilderness Road from the southwestern corner of Virginia to the Cumberland Gap. Blazed along Indian trails and buffalo traces, this was more of a rough path than a road.

Roads were poor in even the well-settled states. From Philadelphia a wagon road went three hundred miles west to Pittsburgh, crossing the Allegheny Mountains. Yet a Philadelphia merchant found it easier and cheaper to send his goods to Pittsburgh by schooner and river boat than to use the overland route. The ship went down the Delaware to the Atlantic Ocean and south to the Gulf of Mexico. At the mouth of the Mississippi, the freight was transferred to a river boat. This boat then moved up the Mississippi and Ohio rivers to Pittsburgh —a distance of more than 3,400 miles.

Forts, trading posts, and villages were soon built along the entire length of the Ohio. Steamboats became numer-

ous in the eighteen-twenties. To the surprise of many settlers, the boats proved that they could travel against the current from New Orleans to Pittsburgh.

The Ohio was only one of the great rivers that opened new land to pioneers. The small rivers were useful, too. Any stream that could float a canoe led men farther into the wilderness.

Trappers, traders, and explorers made the first trails through the little-known land between the Mississippi and the Pacific coast. The only rivers deep enough for boats over long stretches were the Missouri and the Columbia. Most of the emigrants traveled in wagon trains, banding together for protection against Indians. The caravans followed the rivers to avoid as many hills and mountains as possible. On the dry and dusty plains, finding water for men and oxen was often a question of life or death. Rivers with water the year round were scarce. The trails kept close to them.

In the eighteen-thirties canals and railroads were being built faster than money could be found to pay for them. Like many highways, the canals and railroads followed the rivers whenever possible. Often a single valley had one or two highways, a canal, and a railroad. The rivers had worn gentle grades through hills and mountains that would otherwise have been impassable barriers for the canals and railroads. Even today there is hardly an important river without a railroad along its bank.

As the railroad network spread from coast to coast, the canals lost much of their freight business. By the end of the nineteenth century most canals were empty ditches, with trees growing on the towpaths once trod by mules.

Freight and passenger trains took business away from

the river boats, too. But the system of inland waterways has survived because rivers, lakes, and oceans are the cheapest highways in the world. Neither train nor truck nor plane can move a ton of coal as cheaply as a boat can.

River traffic has come a long way from the flatboats of George Washington's time. A diesel-powered towboat two hundred feet long pushes a tow of twenty barges, tied together. The tow is a quarter-mile long. Automobiles are hauled in three-decker barges that carry six hundred cars in the tow. One oil barge carries as much oil as a train of tank cars. A towboat pushes eight of these barges from New Orleans to a refinery on the Ohio.

Today inland waterways have more than ten times as much traffic as they did in 1931. The leading commodity is oil, which accounts for one third of all the tonnage. Next come coal, sand and gravel, lumber, sea shells, and iron and steel. Many more tons are moved over the inland waterways than by all the ships that go to foreign ports.

On the Ohio River, the first steamboats often grounded on sand bars or struck boulders in the river bed. To maintain deep water along the river's 981 miles, the Federal Government has built a chain of forty-six locks and dams. The locks were built when tows were much shorter. A modern towboat with twenty barges must break its tow in half and go through each lock twice. This wastes time and money.

Plans have been made to replace the forty-six locks with nineteen big locks, each twelve hundred feet long. A towboat could then push its tow through with one locking.

Old as rivers are, they adjust wonderfully to modern times. Nothing is more flexible than water.

3 Cities Aren't Accidents

Biloxi, a village on the Gulf of Mexico, expected a great future in the year 1720. The young settlement had been named capital of the French territory of Louisiana, a region larger than Alaska.

But the glory of Biloxi lasted only two years. In 1722 the capital was moved west to a collection of crude huts on the Mississippi River. The new capital had fewer than four hundred people, half of them slaves. Its name was New Orleans.

New Orleans stole the honor from Biloxi with the help of the mighty Mississippi. The river was the main highway to the rich fur country of the upper Mississippi basin and Canada. Its tributary, the Ohio, was a route east to Pennsylvania. The vast western lands were reached by the Missouri, the Red, and other tributaries.

Biloxi had a good harbor. Ships from France could unload colonists and supplies, and take on cargoes of furs and other produce. But Biloxi had no river route to the north country. The Canadian fur traders who came downstream on the Mississippi had to travel a hundred

extra miles east to reach Biloxi.

And so Jean Baptiste Le Moyne, the young French explorer who kept the English out of Louisiana, insisted that New Orleans be made the capital. He knew what geography meant. Today the city on the great river is fifteen times larger than Biloxi. Ocean freighters and river vessels crowd its miles of wharves and docks. Thanks to the Mississippi, New Orleans is the greatest city of the South.

From Louisiana to Minnesota, a chain of cities grew up on the banks of the Mississippi. Baton Rouge, Natchez, Vicksburg, Memphis, Cairo, St. Louis, Quincy, Burlington, Rock Island, Dubuque, La Crosse, St. Paul, and Minneapolis—all began as settlements along the most important inland waterway of the nation.

Settlers built along the Mississippi and other navigable rivers for one main reason: trade. In the beginning trappers pushed out along the rivers and streams into the wilderness. Soon they came back, bringing skins and seeking fresh supplies. This meant trade.

As farmers cleared the land and harvested their crops, trade grew. Meat and wheat went down the Mississippi; sugar and cotton and rice came back. Pittsburgh and other manufacturing centers used the river boats to send tools, guns, and machinery to the new settlements.

More boats on the river meant more business for the towns. Shipmasters bought fuel and provisions. Passengers on the packet boats put many dollars into the pockets of local innkeepers.

Paddle wheelers ruled the Mississippi and Ohio rivers from the early eighteen-twenties until the eighteen-seventies. Hundreds of people were killed by boiler explosions and fires, but boats were the cheapest and quickest way to travel. At first it took twenty-five days to go from New Orleans to Louisville on the Ohio River. Faster boats were built. The trip was cut to four days and nine hours.

Finally the paddle wheelers were put out of business by the railroads. Passenger trains made the run from New Orleans to Louisville in less than twenty-four hours. Railroads haven't stopped barge traffic, of course, for nothing carries a heavy load as cheaply as a boat does. A load of sand or a cargo of oil is usually in no hurry. So a towboat pushes it along the river.

The Mississippi has made New Orleans one of the world's great ports. But it has caused plenty of trouble for the cities in the valley. Floods have taken countless lives and destroyed buildings, highways, and railroads.

Despite the danger, farmers and townspeople have clung to the valley, which is called the world's richest. The Mississippi is their livelihood.

The growth of cities along the Mississippi was to be expected. People settle wherever there is plenty of water. Of the twenty largest cities in the United States, fourteen are on navigable rivers or on bays where navigable rivers provide inland routes. The remaining six cities have ports on the Atlantic or Pacific or on the Great Lakes. It might be said that the most important building material for our big cities has been water.

4
Great Dams

Higher and bigger dams are being built today than were ever dreamed of in years gone by. This period in history might be called the Age of Dams.

Until 1905, no dam in the United States was two hundred feet high. In the next fifty years, 159 dams that high or higher were built or started.

The whole country got excited about Hoover Dam on the Colorado River, completed in 1936. This 726-foot dam created Lake Mead, the largest reservoir in the

United States. The 9,719 billion gallons of Lake Mead could cover the whole state of Virginia a foot deep, with enough left over to give Connecticut a sousing.

Lake Mead ranks seventh among the great reservoirs of the world. Lake Victoria in Uganda and the Bratsk Dam reservoir in the Soviet Union are five times larger.

The new Oroville Dam in California will be four feet higher than Hoover Dam. But Switzerland will set a new world's record when the Grand Dixence Dam is finished. This dam will be 922 feet high.

The great dams of today had small beginnings in pre-historic times. Men have been building dams almost as long as beavers have, which means for thousands of years. The first dams were much like beaver dams: made of stones and earth and branches, and only a few feet high.

These early dams were built by farmers who wanted to irrigate their crops with water from streams or rivers. The farmers went upstream to find a place where the stream could be dammed. There they built the dam, slow-

ing down the stream so that a pond formed. Then they dug canals which carried water from the pond to the fields below.

Over the centuries men learned how to build larger and stronger dams of masonry and concrete. Usually these dams were for a single purpose: either to supply water to a town, or to divert water to turn the wheels of a factory or mill.

Most of the great dams of the United States today are multipurpose dams. One dam may be for irrigation, flood control, electric power production, and water supply. Some dams are planned to make rivers deep enough for barges.

An example of a multipurpose dam is Fort Peck Dam on the Missouri River. It is for irrigation, power, flood control, and navigation. Made of earth, the dam is only 250 feet high—but it is four miles long and the world's biggest dam. The earth in it would fill a train of gondola cars 28,000 miles long. It would take eighty thousand diesel units to pull such a train if the couplings didn't break, which they certainly would.

City populations have grown much faster than rural populations. The average person uses about forty gallons of water each day for drinking, washing, and other personal uses. To keep the pipelines full, some cities have built dams on mountain streams many miles away.

Vast quantities of water are needed in the manufacture of steel, aluminum, paper, chemicals, electricity, and many other products. For example, one paper mill in Houston, Texas, uses 22 million gallons of water a day —twice as much as a city of 100,000 people would use. It takes 65,000 gallons to make a ton of steel, 200,000 gallons for a ton of rayon, 320,000 gallons for a ton of aluminum, and 600,000 gallons for a ton of synthetic rubber.

Twentieth century control of water is something of a miracle. A family in Chicago has cantaloupe for breakfast on a bright morning in June. Part of the juice in the melon may have come from winter snows that fell in Dinosaur National Monument, on the Colorado-Utah border. Spring sunshine melted the snow into the Green River. The river twisted south for hundreds of miles, mostly through desert country. Then it joined the Colorado River, passed through the Grand Canyon, and

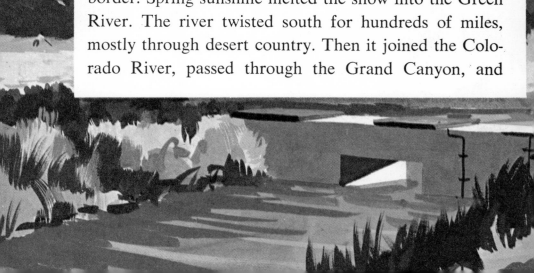

poured into vast Lake Mead.

Sluiceways let the water through Hoover Dam. Many miles south the water was checked by a small dam just above the Mexican border, near Yuma. Here part of the river was turned into the eighty-mile All-American Canal, the biggest irrigation ditch in the country. The canal carried the water through desert sand dunes to the Imperial Valley of California. And there, after passing through a network of ditches, it reached the field where cantaloupes were beginning to swell on vines decked with yellow blossoms.

5
Putting
Rivers
To work

WISE MEN once believed that slaves were necessary. Who else could quarry stone, fell trees, carry burdens, cultivate the fields, and do countless other jobs that called for muscle?

For thousands of years muscle power was the only kind of power used by men. Rich men, politicians, generals, and scholars lived by their wits. The dirty work was done by slaves who had strong backs.

Finally it was discovered that rivers could be used to

do the work of many men. The Egyptians found that running water would turn a big wheel. They fastened pots to the wheel so it would lift water to a trough on the bank. Then the water was used for irrigation.

Paddle wheels were also used to run millstones for grinding grain. When factory machines were invented, many were operated by water power.

In 1882, a new use for water began. At Appleton, Wisconsin, the first hydroelectric station produced electricity from water power. A stream of water rushed down a big pipe and hit the blades of a turbine. The turbine spun rapidly. It turned a dynamo, which generated electricity.

The nation's most famous hydroelectric project was started in 1933. Congress set up the Tennessee Valley Authority, called the TVA, to develop an area as big as England. The valley was in poor shape. Hills had been stripped of trees and good soil washed away. The typical farmhouse was an unpainted shack lit by oil lamps. Water was pumped by hand.

The Tennessee River was a bad actor. Its floods carried away big chunks of the best farm land. Between floods the water was low in the dangerous shoals. Very few boats made the long trip from Paducah, where the river joined the Ohio, to Knoxville—a distance of 650 miles.

TVA put the river to work for the people, instead of against them. It built twenty great dams, improved five existing dams, and took over five more that were privately owned. The thirty dams turned the river into a chain of lakes with locks for river vessels. By 1955, river traffic was fifty times greater than in 1933.

The dams ended the yearly threat of floods. And they provided water for making huge quantities of electric power. The countryside was dark before TVA came to the valley. In Tennessee and Alabama, only one farm out of twenty-five had electricity; in Georgia, one out of thirty-six; in Mississippi, one out of a hundred. Now there is electricity on nine farms out of ten.

Farm kitchens have running water, electric ranges, and

refrigerators. The farmer's wife is no longer a slave. And the farmer is using electricity to milk cows, saw wood, and dry hay.

People in the seven states of the Tennessee Valley use a lot of electricity because it's cheap. The average price of a kilowatt hour in the United States was two and a half cents in 1958. In the TVA region, a kilowatt hour cost about one cent—which was less than half the national average.

Electric rates are kept low because the current is distributed by co-operatives organized by the people themselves. The co-operatives buy electricity at wholesale from TVA.

In the United States, the average family uses 274 kilowatt hours a month. But the average TVA family uses six hundred kilowatt hours a month—more than twice as much. Yet the TVA family pays only $6.42 a month, which is less than the $6.92 average for the whole United States.

Besides taming the river, TVA has worked to rebuild the worn-out land. Farmers have been encouraged to block gullies with dams before the gullies deepen into ravines. TVA nurseries have provided more than 250 million tree seedlings to start forests on worn-out soil.

More than a million families in the valley are living better because a bad river has become their best friend.

6
Lost:
Good Land

SUPPOSE A MILE-LONG TRAIN of gondola cars were filled with mud. Suppose the whole trainload were dumped into the Mississippi River a few miles above St. Louis. Then imagine another trainload being dumped fifteen minutes later. And then another and another, every fifteen minutes throughout the day and night, the whole year round.

That is how much mud the Missouri River has been dumping into the Mississippi a few miles above St. Louis.

37

More than 200 million tons a year, more than 150 tons a minute, almost three tons a second. The Missouri has well earned its nickname of the Big Muddy.

Many thousands of years ago the Missouri River ran north and east and emptied into Hudson Bay. When the glaciers moved down and covered much of northern United States, the Missouri was blocked. Finally it carved a new channel south to the Mississippi.

The Missouri still changes its course frequently, within a "flood plain," the flat area beside the river channel, that is two to fifteen miles wide. George Fitch wrote of the river in 1907:

> It makes farming as fascinating as gambling.
> You never know whether you are going to harvest corn or catfish.

Like every river, the Missouri works in the end to make the land flat. Its enterprise has been aided by Nature and by man. Nature has severely limited the rainfall on the Great Plains. There isn't enough water for forests, ponds, and swamps. The scantily covered soil is easily washed away when the winter snows melt. Hundreds of streams carry mud into rivers that feed the Missouri.

Man has made erosion much worse by plowing under the grass that once fed thousands of buffalo, and by cutting down the few trees and bushes to provide more space for crops. Often you can look for miles without seeing even a small clump of trees. When the winds blow, there are no trees to break their force. The best soil is blown away.

The Mississippi River is already carrying a great deal of silt when the muddy Missouri joins it. More silt means more trouble, all the way to the Gulf of Mexico. Some of the silt settles in the channel, hindering navigation and increasing the risk of floods. Some is carried all the way to the Gulf, where over thousands of years it has built up the Mississippi Delta.

The river spreads out at the delta into three main channels or passes, as they are called by rivermen. The current becomes slower. The silt has more time to settle.

One hundred years ago so much silt had piled up in the passes that ocean-going vessels were being grounded almost every week. They were often stuck for days.

New Orleans was badly worried. If the channel were blocked, the city's trade would be ruined. Engineers tried several plans for clearing the shoals. None worked. Finally, in 1875, Congress turned the problem over to Captain James B. Eads, the man who had built at St. Louis the first bridge across the Mississippi.

Captain Eads built two parallel jetties out of poling, stone, and willow mattresses. He left a two-hundred-foot channel between them. The jetties made the river flow faster. The shoals were gradually washed away.

About one third of all the water emptied into oceans by United States rivers comes from the Mississippi and its tributaries. The average discharge of the Mississippi is about 600,000 cubic feet a second. That much water would fill a train of tank cars three miles long.

A spring flood on the Mississippi sends three or four times the normal amount of water down the valley. Before the white men came, the floodwaters could spread across forty miles of bottom lands. The settlers claimed this rich soil for their farms. They built levees a few feet high to keep the river back. As the levees rose for miles along the lower Mississippi, the river was squeezed into a flow-way ranging from ten miles to only one and a half miles wide. The flood level went much higher—and the levees had to go higher, too.

But the levees were never high enough. Every three or four years the river broke through, flooding hundreds of square miles, washing out roads and houses, drowning people and cattle. In 1912 about two hundred people

were killed. The great flood of 1927 took 310 lives and left 100,000 people homeless. New Orleans was saved only by dynamiting the levee below the city, so the river could spread out on thinly settled land.

After the 1927 flood the Federal Government took on the Mississippi. A plan for preventing bad floods was prepared by the U. S. Army Corps of Engineers. Levees were built or strengthened all the way from the delta to above the Ohio River. The river channel was dredged deeper and wider. In many places it was straightened by digging cutoffs that eliminated horseshoe bends. At five strategic points floodways were planned for emergency use. These openings in the levees would let floodwater escape to lands where it would not do serious damage.

Another bad flood came in 1937. The river was higher

than in 1927. Hodding Carter, newspaper publisher and author of *Lower Mississippi,* wrote:

> I could look from my newspaper office window in Greenville and see the gray Coast Guard cutters seemingly perched upon the levees. The river lapped at the levee top, and the cutters, on hand to aid in rescue work if needed, were moored twenty feet above the ground level of our street.

There were some breaks and some flooding. But the river generally was kept under control.

By 1980, the brown Missouri is expected to be as clear as some of the more respectable rivers in the forested East and North. The 2,714-mile river, longest in the United States, is being given the Tennessee River treatment. The complete plan calls for five huge dams across the Missouri, above Sioux City, making a chain of lakes. There will be 133 other major dams on tributaries.

All of the dams will serve three purposes: flood control, electric power, and irrigation.

Control of the river's flow will stabilize navigation from the junction with the Mississippi to Sioux City, a distance of 762 miles. The plan provides for a channel nine feet deep the whole way, instead of the present three-and-a-half-foot depth for the last 130 miles.

7
Bad Housekeeping

Have you ever seen, close to a good-sized town, a stream that was a delight? I mean a stream with clean pools where trout lurk beneath the rocks; where dragon-flies dart about their business; where the marshy banks are dense with dogtooth violets, ferns, and jack-in-the-pulpits.

Or have you ever seen, near a city, a river that looked and smelled good enough to swim in? A river with a brood of mallard ducklings in pursuit of education, and a great blue heron in pursuit of frogs?

Not in the United States, I am afraid. To find clean streams and rivers in this country, you must go miles from the cities and towns. Most streams in urban areas are hardly better than open sewers. The water is dark and unpleasant, with an oily film.

The stream bed and banks are a dumping ground for every kind of trash—tin cans, bottles, automobile tires, crumpled cartons, broken boards, worn-out shoes, worn-out mattresses, worn-out anything. When you come to a stream in the city, you don't stretch out on the bank and daydream. The view is miserable, and the broken glass doesn't feel good.

A century ago all of the big cities poured their raw sewage into the nearest river or harbor. Scientists warned that this was bad for the public health, especially when drinking water was taken from the same river.

Gradually, methods for treating sewage were developed. Chlorine was used to kill harmful bacteria. Solid matter was kept out of the rivers.

Although we have known for a hundred years how to treat sewage, we have never cleaned up the rivers. We are still polluting rivers, harbors, and ocean beaches with untreated sewage from houses and factories. About twelve thousand municipalities have sewer systems. But only 6,600 have sewage treatment plants—and many of

these are too small to handle the entire flow of sewage.

A survey of 2,600 factories was made by health officials. The U. S. Public Health Service reported that fewer than half had plants for treating their waste water.

The untreated waste from cities and from industry combined is equal to the sewage waste from 150 million people. That is the amount of filth we are pouring into our streams and harbors.

To animals, birds, fishes, and plants, pollution often means death. A wild muskrat was caught several years ago in the river that flows past the atomic plant at Oak Ridge, Tennessee. The muskrat was dying from cancer caused by radioactivity. Small amounts of radioactive waste had been dumped into the stream. Plants at the edge of the water had absorbed these materials through

the water taken up by their roots. The water kept evaporating from the leaves, but the radioactive particles remained, becoming more and more concentrated. The muskrat had eaten the plants. Radioactivity in the bone cancer of the muskrat's right hind leg was 150 times higher than the radioactivity of the water.

Since we have known for a hundred years that untreated waste from houses and factories should not go into streams, we might well ask why it still does. There are two reasons. The first is that sewage treatment costs money. A good municipal plant means a slightly higher tax bill. When a private industrial plant treats its waste, the stockholders get a few cents less in dividends.

The second reason is that we tend to be a sloppy nation. We dump waste almost anywhere, without thought. Candy wrappers fall to the sidewalk, beer cans litter the park, tissues border every highway.

Trash can be swept from the streets. But many of our streams have been ruined beyond repair.

8
A Different World

WALK A HALF MILE from a hilltop to the edge of a river and you have moved to a different world. The change may be greater than if you had crossed the ocean to England or France.

Water makes the difference. Water has its own kinds of plant and animal life. It has also a full share of the plants and animals that live away from rivers. For example, the river is the place to look for muskrats, otters, fish, water snakes, and many water birds. And it is also where you will find opossums, skunks, raccoons, deer, and other animals.

The river is the place for willows, cottonwoods, alders, and reeds. But the banks of a river also invite sycamores, maples, hemlocks, locusts, and a number of other trees.

No river of the United States has more interesting plant and animal life than the Everglades of Florida. And there is no river like the Everglades, which most people think is a vast swamp. Actually, it is a swampy river.

The river runs from Lake Okeechobee south and west to the Gulf of Mexico. It is only one hundred miles long, but it is tremendously wide—from fifty to almost seventy-five miles. The river has no banks. It has no main chan-

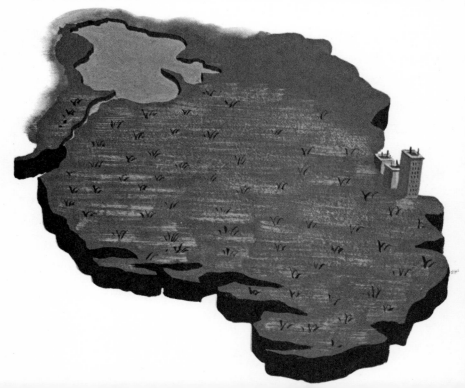

nel and no single mouth. The water is shallow, barely three feet deep in the deepest places. But it moves.

No one has ever followed the river from Okeechobee to the mangrove swamps by the sea. No boat could get through because the river is a sea of grass. This isn't the gentle grass of tidal marshes or sunlit ponds. It is called saw grass but it is actually sedge, not grass. Standing higher than a man's head, the tough blades are folded in the middle and edged with small, sharp teeth.

Through this sea of grass, more than half the size of the state of Connecticut, the river slowly makes its way to the Gulf of Mexico. The current runs faster and the water level rises when the rainy season comes in late August or early September. In a single day twelve inches of rain may fall. The average rainfall in the United States is thirty inches a *year*.

The Everglades is the only tropical region of the United States. In the marshes bordering the river are palms, palmettos, mangroves, live oaks, pines, and cypress trees festooned with the Spanish moss that gets its food from the air. Over thousands of years the decayed vegetation has built up islands and hammocks, covered now with the trees that do not grow in water.

The mortal enemy of the live oak is a rubber tree which belongs to the fig family. If a seed of this rubber tree falls into the bark of a live oak a few feet above

ground, the seed sends hairlike roots downward. The roots thicken and stiffen when they reach the soil. Branches begin their climb to sunlight. Finally the rubber tree encircles and covers the oak with its roots and its shiny leaves. Cut off from the sun, the oak dies.

Like the rubber tree, most animals of the Everglades are killers. The Everglades kite, a hawk, skims the marshes in search of his only meal: snails. The black bear eats nearly everything from fruit to crabs. When he smells turtle eggs buried in the sand, he digs them up. The favorite food of the mountain lion, or cougar, is the little brown deer. The beautiful but poisonous coral snake catches lizards and small snakes.

Since 1947 almost two thousand square miles of the Everglades have been a national park. Federal protection will save many animals and birds threatened by drainage and clearing of the swamps for farms. Alligators, crocodiles, flamingos, and roseate spoonbills will have a better chance.

All rivers spread the seeds of plants and trees, sometimes with the help of birds. Seeds are often carried many miles before they are cast ashore. Some water plants have seeds in buoyant envelopes that the wind helps to push along to a new location. Water birds dig into the slimy, rotten pods of water lilies to find the seeds. A stray seed or two will stick to the bird's bill and finally fall off in another part of the river—or even in a different river.

Insects, spiders, and small animals often travel long distances on rivers without intending to. A tree by the river or a dead branch may fall into the stream, bearing its population of ants, beetles, worms, spiders, and other creatures. Miles downstream the wanderers may find new trees to conquer.

The most famous traveler of rivers is the Pacific salmon. The salmon breed in the headwaters of north Pacific rivers. When the eggs hatch, the young fish go down the river—sometimes hundreds of miles—to reach the ocean and grow up. Several years later the salmon come back to the river where they were born. No other river will do. They fight their way upstream through rapids and over waterfalls to reach the headwaters. The only obstacle that stops them is dams. On the Columbia River, fish ladders (a series of small waterfalls) have been built around every dam so the salmon can get as far as Grand Coulee. After the eggs are laid, the salmon die—and the life cycle begins again.

9
How Much Water Is There?

Water is the cheapest thing we buy. The average price of a ton of water at the kitchen sink is five cents. A ton of milk costs about $250.

Water is cheap because there is plenty of it in most thickly populated areas, and because it comes as a gift of Nature. The only expense is in delivering it from reservoir or well to house, farm, or factory.

Every year about thirty inches of rain falls on the United States. This means that if none of it sank into the ground or evaporated into the air or ran off in rivers, we would be two and a half feet deep in water by New Year's Eve!

Some parts of the country get much more than thirty inches. New Orleans gets sixty-three and Juneau, Alaska, gets ninety, on the average. But Phoenix, in the desert country, averages only seven inches, and some desert regions are even drier.

Three fourths of the rainfall is returned to the air by evaporation. The sun evaporates water from the surface of the ground, from lakes and rivers and ponds, and from the leaves of plants and trees.

One fourth of the rain goes into the ground and runs off into streams and rivers, nearly all of them leading to the ocean. This is the water that fills the reservoirs, that is piped into homes and factories.

Except during heavy rains, rivers get most of their

water from inside the ground, not from the surface. Rain sinks down through the soil to the underlying rock. It may sink down twenty or thirty feet. Indeed, some water may keep going down for hundreds of feet, finding cracks in the rocks or soaking into rocks porous enough to hold water. The rest of the water slowly works its way downhill within the buried rock until it comes to a stream or river or lake. It is water from the ground that keeps rivers flowing during dry spells.

The United States probably has enough land and water to support an even larger population than it now has for many years to come. But we must practice more conservation than we have. For example, federal and local governments have persuaded many owners of hilly farms to adopt contour farming. Instead of planting straight rows up and down a slope, the farmer plants level strips that follow the curve of the hill. Narrow strips of grass are planted at intervals to prevent erosion. Contour farming saves priceless soil and produces better crops. Yet thousands of farmers still run their rows up and down, inviting washouts during heavy rains.

We have known for many years that reckless lumbering is ruinous to watersheds. But some loggers still don't care what happens to the land and water once they get the timber. California provides a shocking example. The finest stand of giant redwoods in the state is the Rockefeller Forest of Humboldt Redwoods State Park. In 1959, a stream called Bull Creek washed out twenty-five trees, all more than three hundred feet tall. These trees were standing before Columbus came to America.

Bull Creek had followed a winding course through the forest for hundreds of years without doing any serious damage. It wasn't a big stream. But in 1947, lumbering began on the creek's watershed above the state park. Fires swept through after the loggers. Nothing was left to hold the rains. Bull Creek became a muddy torrent with a channel two hundred feet wide. The redwoods were undermined.

The western farmers who cultivate every last foot of ground, leaving no tree or bush to check erosion, should take a trip east. They should visit farms in Pennsylvania, Connecticut, and other states. Here the land is seldom cleared completely. Trees are left along the streams and in wood lots. Hedgerows grow up along roads and fences. Some fields are left in grass. These acres don't produce any corn or potatoes, but they help to save soil and water.

Clean rivers are needed to supply drinking water, to serve industry, to irrigate farms, and to keep channels

open for ships. There is a dollar value on all these uses of water.

But there is another value that cannot be figured in dollars. A clean river or stream is a beautiful thing to look at and enjoy. It makes a fine site for a picnic. It becomes a dwelling place for animals, birds, and fishes.

There is one way to make sure that streams in our metropolitan areas are kept clean, with green borders instead of dump heaps. That is by setting aside a strip of land on each side of the stream as a public park.

Of course this would cost money. But it would mean that a hundred years from now there would be clear streams bordered with trees and grass and wild flowers in densely built-up areas. Otherwise our streams will become sewers covered with concrete roofs to hide the filth.

It isn't hard to decide which kind of stream would be best for everybody.

What is a "GISMO"?

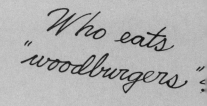

Can you bounce a Ping-pong ball on water?

"Who eats "woodburgers"?

You'll learn about these interesting things in the

Whitman Learn About Books

Have you often wondered about the trees, flowers, and animals that you see in the park or forest? And wouldn't you like to learn about how planes fly, and why a big building goes way down before it goes up? You'll find out about these things, and many others, in the Whitman Learn About Books listed below.

1. THE AIRPORT, OUR LINK TO THE SKY

Tells about radar, instrument landings, strange cargoes, what airport crews, weathermen, and flight crews do.

2. ANIMALS OF THE FIELD AND FOREST

Tells about small animals—skunks, woodchucks, opossums—and big ones—bears, deer, and moose. These and many more. Their food, homes, and habits.

3. BIRDS AROUND US

Learn about how birds fly, how they migrate, why birds build different kinds of nests, and how they feed and train their babies.

4. FLOWERS AND WHAT THEY ARE

Are you sure you know a flower when you see one? Learn about garden and wild flowers, how some flowers got their names, and how they are used for food and fragrance.

5. TREES AND HOW THEY GROW

The story of trees from seed to seed, how trees feed themselves, how leaves turn color. Find out what trees do for man—and who ate "woodburgers."

6. OUR EARTH, WHAT IT IS

Learn about the inside and outside of the earth, what causes volcanoes and earthquakes, how the oceans and mountains came to be.

7. ROCKS AND WHAT THEY TELL US

Find out how rocks tell the story of the earth, why we find fossils of sea animals on mountaintops, what rock paintings tell us about cave men.

8. RIVERS, WHAT THEY DO

Learn about how rivers form, how they cut through mountains, why early pioneer trails, railroads, and even modern roads follow rivers.

9. PHYSICS, ITS MARVELS AND MYSTERIES

Learn about why planes fly, how we see and hear, how to make electricity. Find out how magnetism works and why you can bounce a Ping-pong ball on water.

10. THE BIG BUILDERS

Learn about the "gismo," why the Mohawk Indians work on tall buildings, how skyscrapers, bridges, and dams are built.

The Whitman Learn About Books have been carefully prepared with the editorial assistance of specialists in many fields.